The One You Feed

Josmara Nunez -Morales

Presentation by *BookLeaf Publishing*

Web: www.bookleafpub.com

E-mail: info@bookleafpub.com

ISBN: 9789394788442

First edition 2023

DEDICATION

For the ones who believed in me.

Thank you

Part I:
Shadow (Self)

Part I

The One You Feed

You know I fed the wolf once.
You know, the one which holds malice.
The one who makes you angry and erratic.

My life was moved around like static,
but it was enough not to continue the habit.

Or was it?

Bad Guy

I'll forever be painted as the bad guy.
But indeed, I am.
For allowing you to speak on the defenseless.
By smiling and nodding, I am equally to blame.
I only apologize for the facade I projected. That
everything between us was okay.
It was for your sake, not mine.
To be honest, but you can't be honest!
I never needed a part two.

But I'll forever be the bad guy.

Villains Part I

Their eyes filled with <u>envious</u> anger and their <u>souls</u> filled with <u>hate</u>. They masked themselves like <u>kind</u> hearted <u>people</u> and as someone who could relate.

<u>You</u> finally get to know them, once their mask comes off.
This wasn't them, not <u>even</u> a little bit, not even at all.

But everyone <u>could</u> see how they could <u>damage</u> you, but instead you gave them the chance to consume you.

A couple of years too late, you are already filled with regret from them taking up your space.

You have become the villain <u>yourself</u> over one mistake.

What is the message?

Villains Part II

To the *evil* witch with her *poisoned* apple,
To the lord of the *underworld* who almost turned
me.

To the Sea Witch who almost took my voice
and to the demon who burned me...

You were disguised as characters, it makes it
easier to say
You were all people in my life
Who only knew how to prey.

Part II:
Karma

Imagination

You were disguised as a rainbow.
I imagined you differently.
Betrayal takes many forms.

Two Cents

Being so selfless
Started feeling useless
When it's all over,
The love you had was *worth two cents*.

Carbon Dioxide

You were once the oxygen that filled my lungs
to breathe.
But,
became the poison that filled the air and sucked
the life out of me.

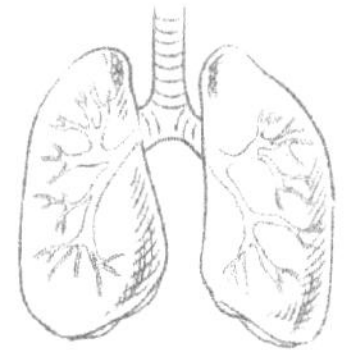

Liar

Your words won't save you
I don't believe you
You will have to show that you have changed
Your words mean nothing.
Show me selflessness
Show me kind

Liar.

Lucky

Maybe you should be afraid of the woman I
have become?
You created her right?

It's unfortunate.

The things I taught you became new things you
taught her.

The experiences we had, new to her.

Oh, how lucky you were to have someone like
me to make you more interesting.

- Laughing out Loud

Over_flow

How did it come to this?

Spoken words, pour out like an *overflowing* bucket of water, I decided to tip it over so that everyone can hear me **scream**.

I'm screaming but no one hears me as everyone doesn't see me, but I am *yelling.* I am yelling so loud that my soul leaves my body but no one can hear me.

I wasn't prepared for this double-edged sword.

I didn't win.

Brewing

Pain is what she feels
Hurt is what she knows.
When everything begins to go wrong
Her anger GROWS...

Shhh....

Fools **Gold**

The luster just makes it look expensive.
But *everyone* can have it because it's free.
It's nothing special, it just looks pretty.
Like *with* some humans that roam this earth, that
have no depth, no heart but *their superficialities*
can get them what they want and people want
them because they are appealing to the eyes.

But many men fall for these fools, and when
they realize it wasn't real, they miss out on the
real value of gold.

Do you see it?

Flames

I should have ripped the whole chapter out of the
book sooner.
The story would have made a lot more sense.
I lit the pages on fire and fanned the flames.
I watched them burn and *smiled*.

It's peaceful here.

Departure

She prepared herself for months before her departure.

The signs were there.

You were too blind to notice.

Part III:
Free (will)

Set Me Free

These words are permanently branded on my skin.
I wanted to fly, but my wings were clipped
I imagined soaring in the sky, seeing my life pass me by
I wondered how different my life would have been
I grew up naive.
I believed that all people had the same heart as me.
Set Me Free

To all the times where men lied to me
It was evident, they had less of a pair than my ovaries.
Set Me Free

From those who loved me so deeply
From those who paid for the others' mistakes
From those who made me feel trapped in which
I cried to be released
Set me Free

From all of the sadness that life brought me
I smiled, but no one knew of the anger that grew inside me.
Set Me Free

From all the memories
They are tainted by the evil I released.
Set me Free
From the friends I had
We hurt one another.
Set Me Free

From all the moments I thought of taking my life
I believed the world would be better off without
me.
Set Me Free

From the loss that I will never get to meet,
From the memories I'll never keep
For all this pain to be released…
Set Me Free
Set Me Free
Set Me Free

I feel Everything

Everything is going in s l o w   m o t i o n
While you just let **chaos** loom over.
What would you do if the world stood still?
The rain on my skin feels warm again.

- Is this what positive emotion feels like?

Knight

It takes a monster to steal your joy,
and a Knight to reclaim it after.

You look familiar

Half/Crazy

I know it's crazy sometimes the predicament we are in.

In love, but so far away

I feel so connected to you.

Romance in 2020

Worthy

"Let me love you." He said.
.

.

.

.

I mean, am I *really* worthy?

I
AM.

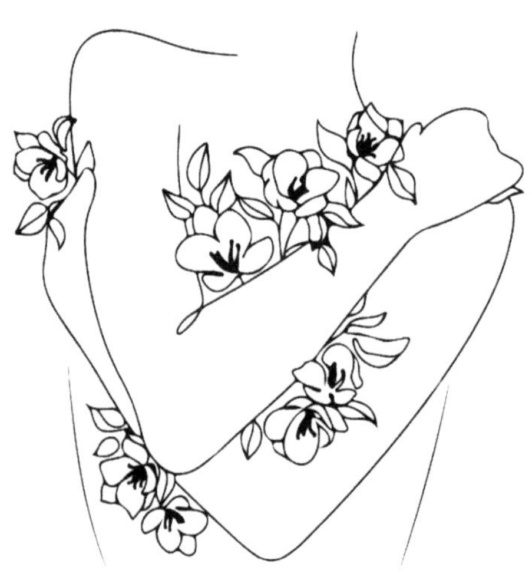

Full Circle

I will admit, my palm said that I wasn't destined
for the happy ending.
All the odds were against me.

Do you remember me back then?

I fed the wrong part of me for a long time.
That anger and hate was not who I truly was.

The *brown-eyed woman* has just come back to
life.

Everything now makes sense.

Full Circle

J.

We built our foundation from stories and
laughter.
I never knew what would come after.
You couldn't tell me that I would find true love
at *twenty-two*.
But as crazy as it sounds, it's always been *you*.

- *My Knight in Shining Armor*

Fin

www.ingramcontent.com/pod-product-compliance
Lightning Source LLC
Chambersburg PA
CBHW051512090625
27923CB00044B/964